Introd

During Holy Week in 1991, Pope John Paul II celebrated the ... , the Cross at the Coliseum in Rome. During that celebration, he omitted some of the traditional stations and added others so that each station was based in Scripture. We are following this new order here.

Thus, the three falls of Jesus, the encounter with his mother before crucifixion, and the meeting with Veronica are all omitted. In their place are key stories from the Gospels about the last days of Jesus' life: the Garden of Olives, the betrayals by Judas and Peter, Pilate's judgment, the scourging, Jesus' final words to the good thief, and his words to Mary and John as they awaited his death.

What is important is that, in praying this wonderful and ancient prayer, we come to grips with the reality of God's love and mercy—and that we come to live differently because of it. In this particular presentation of the Way of the Cross, we are also offered an opportunity to reflect on the work of the Holy Spirit in the modern Church expressed through Pope John XXIII, who called the Second Vatican Council in January of 1959. As we pray here, we unite the final steps of Jesus with the those of Pope John: one inaugurating the reign of God on earth, and the other calling us to fidelity in our mission of proclaiming God's reign in today's world. What a powerful way to pray!

Suggestions for use

In most churches around the world, the tablets or statues depicting the Way of the Cross will not follow the order set down in this new scriptural version. That should not stand in the way however, of the Church's desire to root its divine worship in sacred Scripture.

When using this version in a traditional setting, it is best not to alter Church art but rather to commemorate these stations as though the art depicted them. The effect of the worship will be no less profound.

✤ The First Station ✤

Jesus prays in the Garden of Olives

Leader: We stand in the light of faith…

ALL: And we praise you, O God, for your goodness.

Leader: May our hearts be open to your Word…

ALL: And may our souls be moved by your Spirit.

Remembering the Word (based on Luke 22:39–46)

Leader: Jesus, Lord and Giver of Life, we know that you prayed
in the Garden of Olives for the power to undertake the
difficult work to which God called you. We know that
you loved life and feared death, just as we do. And we
know that your disciples have always found it difficult
to watch and pray at your side, sometimes lacking the
faith to follow your call. May your example of fidelity
guide us as we gradually become the kind of Church of
which you dreamed.

Responsorial Psalm (102:1–4, 8)

ALL: Hear my prayer, Yahweh,
let my cry come to you.
Do not hide your face from me now
for I am in trouble.
Listen to me; answer me quickly when I call.
For my days disappear like smoke,
and my bones burn like a furnace.
My heart is stricken and withered like grass;
I am too wasted to eat my bread.

All day long my enemies taunt me;
those who deride me
use my name like a curse.

Reflection

Leader: In calling the Second Vatican Council, Pope John XXIII challenged the world's Catholics to struggle with many important issues in the Church. Like Jesus in the Garden of Olives, Pope John often prayed to be faithful to what God wants for us. And in the end, Vatican II reformed the Church to more faithfully reflect the mission of Jesus in today's world. For us who are members of this Church today, it is now our task to work diligently to continue this renewal and extend the power of Christ to all the world.

A momentary, sacred pause....

Communal Prayer

ALL: Jesus, we believe in you and we love you. We embrace your presence in our hearts and lives. We accept with gratitude your power to heal and forgive us. We embrace your presence in our Church. Renew it constantly in the vision and energy of your Spirit. Amen.

✤ The Second Station ✤

Jesus is betrayed by Judas

Leader: We stand in the light of faith...

ALL: And we praise you, O God, for your goodness.

Leader: May our hearts be open to your Word...

ALL: And may our souls be moved by your Spirit.

Remembering the Word (based on Matthew 26:45–49)

Leader: Jesus, it's difficult for us to imagine how painful it must
            have been for you to be betrayed to death by one of
            your closest friends. And even more painful must have
            been the form of betrayal: a kiss! And yet you remained
            loving through it all. Judas betrayed you, but the real
            betrayal was of Judas' own self, rejecting his divine call
            to discipleship with you. May your fidelity to love in
            the midst of hate empower us to do likewise and to
            never lose sight of our own divine call.

Responsorial Psalm (37:1–6)

ALL: Do not worry because of wicked people
            and do not be envious of wrongdoers,
            for they will soon fade like grass,
            and wither like green plants.
            Trust in the divine presence and do good deeds.
            In that way you will be at home where you are
            and enjoy security.
            Take delight in the presence of God
            who will give you the desires of your heart.

Commit your way of living to the Spirit.
Trust God who will act.
God will make your virtue shine like the light,
and the right nature of your cause
like the noonday sun.

Reflection

Leader: One of the greatest dangers of modern life is we grow
so accustomed to comfort and security that, without
meaning to, we betray the spirit of the Gospels. Pope
John XXIII was keenly aware of this. Because of his
witness, Vatican II re-emphasized that baptism commits members of the Church to ministry. It commits us
to reach out to others, to love in the midst of hate, to
remain faithful as Jesus did even when he was betrayed
by Judas. And in the end, it commits us to risk even
rejection and security in order to work for justice and
live in peace. For in the end, what matters most is not
financial gain or personal prestige, but that we remain
faithful to Christ.

A momentary, sacred pause....

Communal Prayer

ALL: Jesus, we believe in you and we love you. We embrace
your presence in our hearts and lives. We accept with
gratitude your power to heal and forgive us. We
embrace your presence in our Church. Renew it constantly in the vision and energy of your Spirit. Amen.

✢ The Third Station ✢

Jesus is condemned to death by the Sanhedrin

Leader: We stand in the light of faith...

ALL: And we praise you, O God, for your goodness.

Leader: May our hearts be open to your Word...

ALL: And may our souls be moved by your Spirit.

Remembering the Word (based on Mark 14:56–64)

Leader: Jesus, you stood before the Sanhedrin, a council of your own people, and faced their terrible judgment. They saw you, but rejected your word of love and your life-style of repentance and faith. They did not believe in your healing and teaching power. And they did not see the very face of God in your face. May we ourselves, here and now, stop judging one another likewise. May we instead see the face of God in the faces of all around us, even those we find most difficult to love.

Responsorial Psalm (36:1–4)

ALL: Sinners listen to evil deep in their hearts;
they have no awe in the face of divine presence.
For they lie to themselves so well
that they can no longer recognize or hate
their own sin.
Whatever they say is foolish or false.
They have ceased to act wisely and do good.
They plot their sins
while lying awake at night.

I tell you, they are set on a way that is horrible
and they do not reject evil.

Reflection

Leader: It was one of Pope John's dreams that Vatican II would
open the windows and the doors of the Church again.
For many centuries, the Church's doors had been
closed and the leaders of the Church had been in the
business of judging others, of deciding who was worthy
to receive God's love and who was not. Like Jesus,
many people were judged harshly during those years.
But now the Church sees itself as a loving sign of the
reign of God on earth. God, we know, loves all without
distinction. As such, the Church now embraces all who
come to join in the banquet.

A momentary, sacred pause....

Communal Prayer

ALL: Jesus, we believe in you and we love you. We embrace
your presence in our hearts and lives. We accept with
gratitude your power to heal and forgive us. We
embrace your presence in our Church. Renew it constantly in the vision and energy of your Spirit. Amen.

✣ The Fourth Station ✣

Jesus is denied by Peter

Leader: We stand in the light of faith...

ALL: And we praise you, O God, for your goodness.

Leader: May our hearts be open to your Word...

ALL: And may our souls be moved by your Spirit.

Remembering the Word (based on Luke 22:54–62)

Leader: Jesus, we know that you suffered much rejection and much hatred for being the person God had called you to be. We know that when people around you saw love, they rejected it—and you with it! But what could have been more painful for you than the rejection of Peter? He was the one you had chosen, the one you had taught, and the one you had loved so deeply. May we risk this same kind of rejection as we stand up for justice, for what is right, for those who are living as God calls them to live.

Responsorial Psalm (38:1–4)

ALL: Oh God, do not punish me in your anger,
or discipline me in your rage.
For your arrows have pierced me,
and your hand has come down on me.
I experience no wholeness in my body
because of your fury;
I am unhealthy to my very bones;
it is all because of my sin.
For my sinning has now overwhelmed me

and weighs me down.

It is a burden which is too heavy for me.

Reflection

Leader: Many people in today's world live on the fringe of life. They have come to a decision in life and, after careful thought and prayer, they have chosen to follow their conscience—even when it flies in the face of social custom. They have gotten involved in the justice and peace movement; they have chosen to live simply rather than spend extravagently; or they have opposed unjust corporate or ecclesial behavior.

At Vatican II, the bishops of the world, along with Pope John, understood once again the role of our consciences in deciding how we will live the Christian life. Our conscience, they said, is that place where we are alone with God, that final place where we must accept or reject Jesus as we know him. Just as Peter rejected Jesus, so we sometimes reject those who follow their well-formed consciences.

A momentary, sacred pause....

Communal Prayer

ALL: Jesus, we believe in you and we love you. We embrace your presence in our hearts and lives. We accept with gratitude your power to heal and forgive us. We embrace your presence in our Church. Renew it constantly in the vision and energy of your Spirit. Amen.

✠ The Fifth Station ✠

Jesus is judged by Pilate

Leader: We stand in the light of faith…

ALL: And we praise you, O God, for your goodness.

Leader: May our hearts be open to your Word…

ALL: And may our souls be moved by your Spirit.

Remembering the Word (based on Luke 23:20–25)

Leader: Jesus, whatever went on between you and Pilate there
            on that day of your judgment, we do not know. But we
            do know that throughout it all you remained faithful to
            yourself. You stood in the midst of a society of fear,
            anger, and aggression—but you stood there as a person
            of peace, love, and faith. May we also stand upright at
            the time of our own judgment in society. May we have
            your courage and the strength of your soul when we
            ourselves are faced with anger, fear, and aggression.

Responsorial Psalm (35:15–20)

ALL: The crowd now gathers together
            and is happy that I have fallen.
            They mock me:
            many of them I don't even know!
            They scream at me and ridicule me,
            grinding their teeth at me in hatred.
            How long, Oh God, will you permit this?
            Rescue me from these horrid beasts
            and save me from these lions!

Then I will thank you in the assembly;

in the mighty throng I will praise you.

Do not let my treacherous enemies rejoice over me,

or permit the sly wink of those who hate me.

For they do not speak peace,

but they make up lies against those who are innocent,

the ones causing no harm among us.

Reflection

Leader: It is inescapable that Christians are called to a life in which there is the risk of rejection. When we follow Jesus faithfully, we live in such a way that society around us will be threatened. Those who have chosen to live with fear, anger, and aggression will see love in us and reject it. They will not be able to see through it to find Christ.

This was Pope John XXIII's dream: that we would replace hatred and division with love, despite the cost. When Vatican II called us to activity in the world, it was calling us to this radical form of love. Many times, therefore, when we work for justice, love, peace, and goodness we will ironically encounter the terrible judgments of people like Pilate, people who know better but don't have the courage to support us publicly.

A momentary, sacred pause....

Communal Prayer

ALL: Jesus, we believe in you and we love you. We embrace your presence in our hearts and lives. We accept with gratitude your power to heal and forgive us. We embrace your presence in our Church. Renew it constantly in the vision and energy of your Spirit. Amen.

✠ The Sixth Station ✠

Jesus is flogged and crowned with thorns

Leader: We stand in the light of faith...

ALL: And we praise you, O God, for your goodness.

Leader: May our hearts be open to your Word...

ALL: And may our souls be moved by your Spirit.

Remembering the Word (based on John 19:1–3)

Leader: Jesus, we have already walked with you through judgment and condemnation. Now we stand as witnesses
while you are beaten and mocked, all in the name of
religious righteousness. How can this go on? How can
people hurt each other so violently? May we who have
the power to hurt others—which is all of us—refuse to
do so. May we become women and men of love instead.

Responsorial Psalm (27:1–3, 13–14)

ALL: God is my enlightenment and my healing:
whom shall I fear?
God is the stronghold of my life;
of whom shall I be afraid?
When evil people attack me
to hurt or even kill me,
they are the ones who stumble and fall.
Even if an entire army would attack me this way,
my heart would not fear;
a full scale war could rise up against me,
but I would still be confident!

I believe I shall see the goodness of God
in the land of the living.
Trust in God!
Be strong and let your heart take courage;
I tell you again: trust in God.

Reflection

Leader: How easy it is for us to turn on one another, even on people we love, in small but biting ways. How easy for us to mock each other, to "beat" one another with complaints, meanness, and criticisms. In his journal, Pope John spoke about how difficult it is to accept the unkindness of others while remaining charitable ourselves. But he also knew how essential it is for us on the Christian journey to do so. Vatican II urged us to live in peace and love with each other. Recognizing that the reign of God can be established only when such peace prevails, they sounded a loud call for all of us to live lives of holiness, which means lives where we avoid treating each other as Christ was treated by the soldiers. It means we should go out of our way to affirm and support each other instead.

A momentary, sacred pause....

Communal Prayer

ALL: Jesus, we believe in you and we love you. We embrace your presence in our hearts and lives. We accept with gratitude your power to heal and forgive us. We embrace your presence in our Church. Renew it constantly in the vision and energy of your Spirit. Amen.

✤ The Seventh Station ✤

Jesus carries his cross

Leader: We stand in the light of faith…

ALL: And we praise you, O God, for your goodness.

Leader: May our hearts be open to your Word…

ALL: And may our souls be moved by your Spirit.

Remembering the Word (based on John 19:17)

Leader: Jesus, you are on a terrible journey, a path through
            darkness. How could you trust in God when the events
            of your life are crashing down around you? How could
            anyone believe that God is gracious when death awaits
            at the end of the road? But it was just at this point in
            your journey of faith where you showed the most
            courage and strength. You knew God had not aban-
            doned you, that you still lived in love. And you knew
            this journey would bring you to life everlasting. Jesus,
            may we likewise be willing to bear with one another all
            the needs of the modern world. May we be moved to
            work with the poor, to visit the imprisoned, to fight for
            justice at every occasion possible, and to lead the
            march for peace.

Responsorial Psalm (77:1–2, 5–8)

ALL: I cry aloud to God,
            aloud to God I cry that God may hear me.
            When I am in trouble I seek God.
            Throughout the night I stretch out my hand
            but my soul refuses to be comforted.

I think about the old days,

and remember years past.

All night long I am preoccupied with this;

I meditate and ask myself:

Will God reject me forever?

Will God never again be favorable to me?

Has God's unconditional love ceased forever?

Are God's promises ended for all time?

Reflection

Leader: Pope John XXIII knew he was dying more than a year
before his actual death. Like Jesus, he loved life and
did not want to die. The Second Vatican Council had
just opened and he had hoped to see its work complet-
ed. But also like Jesus, Pope John allowed his impend-
ing death to shape his life. It was only after he was told
how serious his cancer was that he undertook the writ-
ing of some of his most important work. And, in the
end, Vatican II remained faithful to Pope John's spirit
even after his death. It reformed the Church to prepare
it for ministry in the modern world.

A momentary, sacred pause....

Communal Prayer

ALL: Jesus, we believe in you and we love you. We embrace
your presence in our hearts and lives. We accept with
gratitude your power to heal and forgive us. We
embrace your presence in our Church. Renew it constantly in the vision and energy of your Spirit. Amen.

✜ The Eighth Station ✜

Jesus is helped by Simon of Cyrene

Leader: We stand in the light of faith…

ALL: And we praise you, O God, for your goodness.

Leader: May our hearts be open to your Word…

ALL: And may our souls be moved by your Spirit.

Remembering the Word (based on Mark 15:20–21)

Leader: Jesus, we remember how generous you were to those around you during your life, how you touched and healed all who came asking for help. We remember as well the power of your presence and the astonishment of the crowds when they heard your teaching. You led the people to freedom and guided them to know their own souls. So here in this moment on your way to the cross, you received the help of someone else, a stranger to you: Simon. May we likewise receive help when we most need it.

Responsorial Psalm (86:1–7)

ALL: O God, listen to me and answer me,

for I am poor and needy.

Preserve my life, for I am loyal to you;

save me because I am your servant

and I trust in you.

You are my God; show mercy toward me

because you are the only one to whom I pray.

Give me reason to celebrate,

for to you, O God, I lift my soul.

You, O God, are good and forgiving,

abounding in faithful love

for all who pray to you.

So listen, O God, to my prayer;

listen to my cry for help!

When I am in trouble I call on you,

for you will answer me.

Reflection

Leader: For many centuries, it was the central concern of the Church that each member should care for and save his or her soul. But at Vatican II the focus of how we reach salvation shifted. Now we are concerned with helping to establish the reign of God on earth. We seek to animate the world with the Spirit of Christ. It was Pope John's desire that all Christians—Catholic, Protestant, or Anglican—come together to do this work. He sought an end to the barriers that once divided us. So it is no longer our own souls that we seek to save. Just as Simon helped Jesus on his way, so we, too, are called to help one another.

A momentary, sacred pause....

Communal Prayer

ALL: Jesus, we believe in you and we love you. We embrace your presence in our hearts and lives. We accept with gratitude your power to heal and forgive us. We embrace your presence in our Church. Renew it constantly in the vision and energy of your Spirit. Amen.

✤ The Ninth Station ✤

Jesus encounters the women of Jerusalem

Leader: We stand in the light of faith…

ALL: And we praise you, O God, for your goodness.

Leader: May our hearts be open to your Word…

ALL: And may our souls be moved by your Spirit.

Remembering the Word (based on Luke 23:27–31)

Leader: Jesus, we know that many women joined your compa-
            ny of apostles. We know much of your ministry was
            financed by some of the wealthy women who believed
            in you. And we know that it was to a woman—Mary of
            Magdala—that you first revealed your resurrection. So
            it is to these women of Jerusalem that you give one of
            your last teachings: a call to repentance. May we hear
            that call ourselves now. May we accept you and follow
            your way.

Responsorial Psalm (91:1–7)

ALL: If you allow the Most High to be your shelter
            and stay close to the Almighty One
            then you can say to God:
            "You are indeed my refuge and my fortress;
            you are my God. I trust in you."
            For God will rescue you from the trap
            set by the deadly hunter
            and save you from the deadly plague.
            God will cover you with protective feathers

and under those wings you will find safety.

God's fidelity to you is a shield and protector.

You needn't fear the terrors of night,

or the arrow that flies by day,

not the pestilence that stalks in secret,

or the destruction that comes in broad daylight.

A thousand may fall at your side,

ten thousand at your right hand,

but you will be safe forever!

Reflection

Leader: In bringing together the people of the Church for Vatican II, Pope John hoped to open hearts to the Spirit alive in the world today, and thus help all people come to know Jesus and the salvation he offers us. The "final warning" which Jesus gave to the women of Jerusalem, Pope John knew, might have been given to us: watch out! If you live in selfishness and violence then even greater evils will come upon you. If you do not become peacemakers, then you can expect war. And if you do not embrace God's will for you today, then you will live outside the reign of God.

A momentary, sacred pause....

Communal Prayer

ALL: Jesus, we believe in you and we love you. We embrace your presence in our hearts and lives. We accept with gratitude your power to heal and forgive us. We embrace your presence in our Church. Renew it constantly in the vision and energy of your Spirit. Amen.

✤ The Tenth Station ✤

Jesus is crucified

Leader: We stand in the light of faith...

ALL: And we praise you, O God, for your goodness.

Leader: May our hearts be open to your Word...

ALL: And may our souls be moved by your Spirit.

Remembering the Word (based on Mark 15:22–26)

Leader: Jesus, your insight and understanding of what God wants for us and for the world was so firm, so clear, and so deep within you that you could do nothing other than allow yourself to be crucified for it. Your mission was in such direct opposition to the forces of your culture and Church. Your vision drove you to radical belief. May we possess even a fraction of that dedication. May we believe with the same conviction that empowered you.

Responsorial Psalm (22:1–4, 16–19)

ALL   My God, my God, why have you deserted me?

Why are you so distant from helping me,

from the words of my plea?

O my God, I spend the whole day pleading

but you give me no answer;

And I pray at night, but still I find no rest.

Yet you are holy,

a home where Israel sings its praises.

In you our ancestors trusted;

they trusted, and you remained with them.

A company of evildoers encircles me.

My hands and feet have shriveled;

I can count all my bones.

My enemies stare and gloat over me;

they divide my clothes among themselves,

and for my clothing they cast lots.

O God, do not be far away!

O my help, come quickly to my aid!

Reflection

Leader: The vocation of the Christian man or woman has a new focus since Pope John called the world to a clearer vision of justice. Where once it was enough for us to give a few nickels in charity for the poor, we Christians now realize more fully that we are called by baptism to change the systems that make people poor. Even when they are larger and more powerful than we, we are still called to fight for the reform of these systems until the poor see justice. Very few of us have made this teaching of Vatican II our own. We are so busy with our own lives on a day-to-day basis that the poor get ignored. In a word, they are crucified with Jesus on the cross of our indifference.

A momentary, sacred pause....

Communal Prayer

ALL: Jesus, we believe in you and we love you. We embrace your presence in our hearts and lives. We accept with gratitude your power to heal and forgive us. We embrace your presence in our Church. Renew it constantly in the vision and energy of your Spirit. Amen.

✤ The Eleventh Station ✤

Jesus promises to share his reign with the good thief

Leader: We stand in the light of faith...

ALL: And we praise you, O God, for your goodness.

Leader: May our hearts be open to your Word...

ALL: And may our souls be moved by your Spirit.

Remembering the Word (based on Luke 23:39–43)

Leader: Jesus, the clarity of your vision allowed you to recognize goodness even in the midst of hate and evil. And your ever present charity allowed you to offer love in the midst of violence and death. In offering forgiveness and kindness to the criminal crucified with you, you extended the reign of God to all who seem initially to be living outside your reign. May we also be attentive to goodness in this way, and may we also offer love in the face of hate. And may our Church become a haven for the unwanted and unloved.

Responsorial Psalm (25:1–5)

ALL: To you O God, I lift up my soul.

O my God, in you I trust;

do not let me be put to shame;

do not let my enemies gloat over me.

Do not let those who trust in you be put to shame;

let them be ashamed who are freely sinful!

Enlighten me so I may know your ways, O God;

teach me your paths.

Lead me in your truth,

for you are the God who saves me.

You are the one in whom I hope forever!

Reflection

Leader: There was a time in the Christian Church when all those who did not believe as we did were considered incapable of ever reaching heaven. These outsiders were considered sinners and heretics—and sometimes they were hounded out of our communities or even killed in the name of Christ. Many of these people were Jews, but they might also have been Muslims, Buddhists, Native peoples, or others.

In calling Vatican II, Pope John explicitly included everyone, Catholic or not, in his embrace. He considered all people precious and loved children of God. The council itself echoed Pope John's spirit and eventually wrote that all people of good faith, no matter what that faith is, are worthy of God's love—and ours as well.

A momentary, sacred pause....

Communal Prayer

ALL: Jesus, we believe in you and we love you. We embrace your presence in our hearts and lives. We accept with gratitude your power to heal and forgive us. We embrace your presence in our Church. Renew it constantly in the vision and energy of your Spirit. Amen.

✤ The Twelfth Station ✤

Jesus is on the cross with his mother and disciple below

Leader: We stand in the light of faith...

ALL: And we praise you, O God, for your goodness.

Leader: May our hearts be open to your Word...

ALL: And may our souls be moved by your Spirit.

Remembering the Word (based on John 19:25–27)

Leader: Jesus, we are given to one another for love and care, just as you loved and cared for your mother, Mary, even while dying yourself. In asking Mary and John to care for each other as mother and son, you were giving us an example: may we become each other's mothers, fathers, sons, and daughters ourselves. May we become the family of God! May we keep one another safe from harm and hold one another fast in the storms of life. And may we trust that your divine Spirit gives us the power to do this.

Responsorial Psalm (121)

ALL: I stand, looking up to the hills asking,
"From where will my help come?"
My help comes from God
who made heaven and earth.
God will not let your foot slip on the path,
the One who keeps you will never rest!
The One who keeps Israel
will neither slumber nor sleep.

God is your keeper; God is your shade:
the sun shall not burn you by day,
nor the moon harm you by night.
God will keep you from all harm;
God keeps your life.
God accompanies you
whether you are going out or coming in,
now and forever!

Reflection

Leader: While it is true that Vatican II called us all to care for the men and women of the world who suffer and are in pain, we know it is impossible for most of us to leave our homes and do that in person. But there is another call that is closer to home, a call to take care of each other right here in the parish to which we belong. The Eucharist we share makes us the Body of Christ. It unites us. It does for us what Jesus did for Mary and John from the cross: it places us in each other's care. Through us, God cares for our neighbors and friends in this parish. God indeed is our keeper, but we are God's hands and feet.

A momentary, sacred pause....

Communal Prayer

ALL: Jesus, we believe in you and we love you. We embrace your presence in our hearts and lives. We accept with gratitude your power to heal and forgive us. We embrace your presence in our Church. Renew it constantly in the vision and energy of your Spirit. Amen.

✤ The Thirteenth Station ✤

Jesus dies on the cross

Leader: We stand in the light of faith...

ALL: And we praise you, O God, for your goodness.

Leader: May our hearts be open to your Word...

ALL: And may our souls be moved by your Spirit.

Remembering the Word (based on Matthew 27:45–50)

Leader: Jesus, we believe in you and we love you. We have been moved by your powerful presence among us and we have entered into your death ourselves, seeking to find in you the source of our life and love. May we freely give of our own lives for one another. May we be filled with the power of your grace.

Responsorial Psalm (130)

ALL: Out of the depths I cry to you, O God!
            O God, hear me when I call!
            Listen with compassion
            to my plea for mercy!
            If you, O God, remember our sins,
            who could ever stand?
            But you do indeed offer us forgiveness
            and we honor you for that.
            I trust in you, O God.
            My soul trusts your word.
            I have more trust in you to be present
            than those who wait for dawn.

O members of the church,

let us hope in God

more than those who watch for morning!

For with God there is steadfast love,

and with God there is great power to heal.

It is God who will redeem us

from all our sins.

Reflection

Leader: As he was preparing to die himself, Pope John told his closest friends not to worry about him because, he said, his bags were packed! Like Jesus, Pope John trusted that God would not abandon him. Let us pause on our way of the cross to allow the reality of Jesus to enter deeply into our own souls.

A momentary, sacred pause....

Communal Prayer

ALL: Jesus, we believe in you and we love you. We embrace your presence in our hearts and lives. We accept with gratitude your power to heal and forgive us. We embrace your presence in our Church. Renew it constantly in the vision and energy of your Spirit. Amen.

✣ The Fourteenth Station ✣

Jesus is placed in the tomb

Leader: We stand in the light of faith...

ALL: And we praise you, O God, for your goodness.

Leader: May our hearts be open to your Word...

ALL: And may our souls be moved by your Spirit.

Remembering the Word (based on Matthew 27:57–61)

Leader: Jesus, our few moments here remembering your final days and nights are ending, as you are being placed in the tomb by friends who loved you and believed in you. This journey for us has taken us back to your betrayals, trials, and violent death. We do not pretend to understand all these mysteries, but we do now see the connection between your journey and our own. May we remain conscious of your presence among us now so that we are always aware of our own power to teach, heal, and minister in your name. Amen.

Responsorial Psalm (23)

ALL: O God, you are my shepherd,
I lack nothing whatsoever!
You give me rest in green pastures.
You lead me beside still waters; you restore my soul.
You guide me in ways that are right
for your name's sake.
Even though I walk through the darkest valley,
I fear no evil for you are with me;
your rod and your staff comfort me.

You prepare a table before me
in the presence of my enemies;
you anoint my head with oil; my cup overflows.
Surely goodness and mercy shall follow me
all the days of my life
and I shall dwell in your house forever!

Reflection

Leader: In calling Vatican II, Pope John knew the Spirit would be with the Church and that the Risen Christ would empower the Church to reform itself dramatically. Pope John dreamed of releasing to the world the saving and life-giving salvation of Jesus Christ. He hoped to make the world a more holy place, less filled with laws and regulations intended to keep us close to God, and more filled with well-formed hearts and souls, eager to know God and to spread the word. Vatican II refocused us. Our real mission is not to develop effective and well-financed parishes; it is to release into the world the powerful Spirit of Jesus. Let us now go about our work in the Church and the world aware of the connection and indeed, determined to spread the Word.

A momentary, sacred pause....

Communal Prayer

ALL: Jesus, we believe in you and we love you. We embrace your presence in our hearts and lives. We accept with gratitude your power to heal and forgive us. We embrace your presence in our Church. Renew it constantly in the vision and energy of your Spirit. Amen.

✤ The Fifteenth Station ✤

Jesus is raised from the dead

Reflection

There was never anyone like Pope John in the entire history of the Church. Standing in the very place occupied by so many of his predecessors, he could see beyond them all. In speaking of his reasons for calling Vatican II, he once said, "We must shake off the imperial dust that has accumulated on the throne of St. Peter since Constantine" in the fourth century.

Two thousand years ago, the first members of the Church stood there in the tomb looking for the Jesus they had known so well. They were looking for the fellow with whom they had broken bread so often. But what was the message they heard? "Why," they were asked, "do you seek the living here, among the dead?"

In the spirit of good Pope John, we, too, must stop looking among the dead for that which is living in the Church. We must embrace the work of the Spirit as it unfolds around us. We must seek life for the Church by looking forward, not backward. May we seek the living in the fresh gifts of the Spirit, ever poured out on the Church.

A momentary, sacred pause....

Communal Prayer

Jesus, we believe in you and we love you. We embrace your presence in our hearts and lives. We accept with gratitude your power to heal and forgive us. We embrace your presence in our Church. Renew it constantly in the vision and energy of your Spirit. Amen.

XXIII TWENTY-THIRD PUBLICATIONS
P.O. Box 180 • Mystic, CT 06355 • 1-800-321-0411